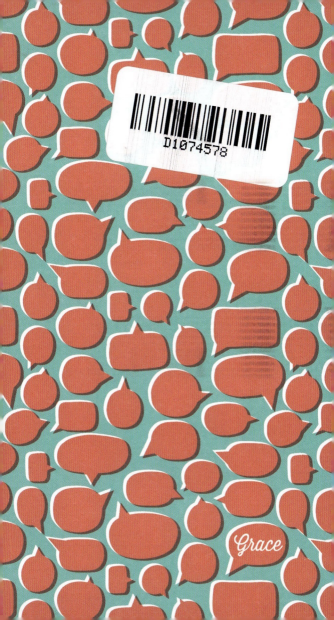

Grace

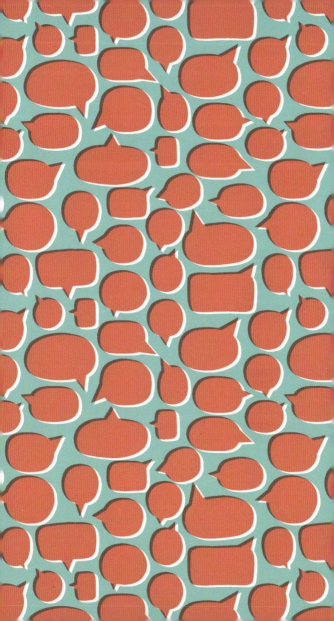

To

_____

From

_____

Date

_____

Say GRACE

50 Life Lessons from Mama

DaySpring

LIVE YOUR FAITH

Say Grace: 50 Life Lessons from Mama
Copyright © 2020 by DaySpring Cards, Inc.
First Edition, November 2020

Published by:

21154 Highway 16 East
Siloam Springs, AR 72761
dayspring.com

Written by: Anita Higman
Cover Design: Jessica Wei

Printed in China
Prime: J2431
ISBN: 978-1-64454-810-3

Contents

Dedication

To my dumpling darling grandbaby,
Freya Nicole. You have stolen my heart.
I love you ever-so-dearly, and I'm looking
forward to watching you grow up!

ANITA HIGMAN
ALSO KNOWN AS GIGI (GRANDMA)

Introduction

Mamas live for the words "I love you!" But beyond that bliss, the most welcome words to a mother's ears are, "Wow, Mama, you were right all along!" Moms yearn for those words—I know I do—because we hope to offer our kids a valuable assortment of commonsense-isms along with generous helpings from God's good Word. You know, to help them to stumble less, laugh more, and come to know that the Lord's love is warmer than sunshine, more refreshing than a clear-running creek, and sweeter than the best Southern tea!

I hope you are delighted with this collection of devotions, which were inspired from various "Southern sayings from Mama." My prayer is that they will warm your heart, draw you closer to the Lord, and maybe even give you a grin and a giggle.

ANITA HIGMAN

Honey Child!

Wondrously show your steadfast love,
O Savior of those who seek refuge from
their adversaries at your right hand.
Keep me as the apple of your eye; hide
me in the shadow of your wings.

PSALM 17:7–8 (ESV)

From the moment your baby curls her chubby, dimpled hand around yours, and she melts your heart like butter on warm biscuits, well, admit it—you're a goner. And right away you begin the merry business of trying to come up with sweet little nicknames for her. Like sugar booger, kitty-poo, potato cakes, punkin-face, wiggle-bum, or maybe booper! Some terms of endearment are obviously more eye-blinking than others. But some are merely precious with a Southern flair—like honey child. Ahh, now we can all agree on that one. When it comes to creating affectionate pet names, we just can't help ourselves. We are, in fact, head-over-heels in love with our babies.

And so it goes with God and each and every one of us. In fact, God is so in love with us, He calls us the apple of His eye. Isn't that lovely? That shows how cherished we are to Him. It reveals the lavishness of His affections towards us.

And if that isn't enough, we are told in Exodus 19:4–5 that we are called His treasured possessions. "You yourselves have seen what I did to the Egyptians, and how I bore you on eagles' wings and brought you to myself. Now therefore, if you will indeed obey my voice and keep my covenant, you shall be my treasured possession among all peoples, for all the earth is mine" (ESV). This beautiful familial kind of love note is not just written for the Israelites, but for me—and for you. Oh yes, the loving ways of God. Who can fathom them?

> GOD IS SO IN LOVE WITH US, HE CALLS US THE APPLE OF HIS EYE. DON'T YOU JUST LOVE THAT?

Lord God, I don't understand why You love me so much, but I am so grateful that You do. I love reading about all Your sweet terms of endearment. Please show me how I can love You back with the same fervency, and help me to reflect that love to a hurting world! Amen.

You Can Catch More Flies with Honey than Vinegar

*A soft and gentle and thoughtful
answer turns away wrath,
but harsh and painful and
careless words stir up anger.*

PROVERBS 15:1 (AMP)

Julianna's male boss was kind of big and boxy looking, and he kind of clomped and lumbered around, so employees liked to call him Frankenstein behind his back. They thought about calling him Bigfoot but that was too charitable. Some people wanted to feel sorry for the guy, but they couldn't quite get there. Like King Belshazzar in the book of Daniel, when the boss man got weighed, he always came up wanting in spite of his monstrous bulk. In the end, it was always a matter of heart. He had such a small one, and he didn't much like to use it. So, he went around squawking harsh comments and flinging careless putdowns and shooting miserable little sneers at people for no other reason than he or she was standing in his path. The man was a miserable mess, and he stirred up trouble everywhere he went. People didn't know what to do with him. They complained. They yelled back. They seethed with inner rage. They developed ulcers. They got counseling. They sometimes prayed. Some employees even quit and went to work for someone who knew how to behave properly. Julianna always knew the man's "carrying on" was excessive and needless. The boss could have calmed himself and replied with reason. With a visit to the little book of Proverbs he could have learned big things.

> HOW MANY OF US HAVE BEEN A MISERABLE MESS AT TIMES AND WE DON'T EVEN KNOW IT?

How many of us have been a miserable mess at times and we didn't even know it? How many folks have secretly wanted to call us Frankenstein—or worse? May we all make frequent visits to a book in the Bible that is filled with great advice—Proverbs.

Father God, sometimes when I get overwhelmed with life and I get flustered with people, I turn into a monster. Please help me to not stir up anger, but to respond to people in a way that would please You. In Jesus' holy name I pray. Amen.

Might as Well Be Talking to a Brick Wall!

Whoever does not welcome you,
nor listen to your message,
as you leave that house or city,
shake the dust [of it] off your feet
[in contempt, breaking all ties].

MATTHEW 10:14 (AMP)

Have you ever tried sharing something important, and when you were finished making your well-articulated point, the other person just stood gaping at you like you were an intelligent life form from another planet—only without the intelligence? But wait, you were so stirring and eloquent! Then, if you kept re-explaining your viewpoint, desperate to be understood, your attempts just spiraled off into a black hole? Rats. It became obvious that they hoped you'd head back to the mother ship. Yeah, everybody has known that "talking to a brick wall" effect that Mama told you about.

And when it comes to sharing the Good News of the gospel, well, some folks hear your gentle witness about Christ and respond in a positive way, and others look at you like you're that same alien creature from outer space. This latter response might mean that—for now—you need to lovingly back away. Should you keep praying for those who are hurting and broken and soul-needy, even when they turn

YEAH, EVERYBODY HAS KNOWN THAT "TALKING TO A BRICK WALL" EFFECT THAT MAMA TOLD YOU ABOUT.

you away? Absolutely. Always hope. Always pray. Always love. For that is the way of our Lord . . .

Jesus, when I share the Good News, please help me to have enthusiasm, and wisdom, and love. I know that You want no one to perish and for all to come to know You as Lord, so please through the power of Your Holy Spirit show me how to be the right kind of witness—when to keep listening and sharing and when to leave them in Your holy hands. For I know You love them even more than I do! Amen.

You Are Cute as a Button

*When they saw it, they made known
the saying that had been told them
concerning this child. And all who heard
it wondered at what the shepherds told
them. But Mary treasured up all these
things, pondering them in her heart.*

LUKE 2:17–19 (ESV)

As a baby, Mama whispered soft kisses across your head and tummy and toes, and you giggled and cooed and burbled tiny bubbles. Adorable. Mama couldn't help it, you see, since you were as cute as a button.

When reading about Jesus' mother, Mary, it's impossible not to wonder about the myriad thoughts about her first baby. After all, she was carrying in her womb and then later in her arms the Creator of the universe! We would naturally assume that Jesus would arrive as a beautiful baby and then grow up to be handsome and bright and royal looking. However, we are told a fascinating fact about Jesus in Isaiah 53:1–3. It reads, "Who has believed what we have heard? And to whom has the arm of the Lord been revealed? For He grew up before Him like a young plant, and like a root out of dry ground; He had no form or majesty that we should look at Him, nothing in His appearance that we should desire Him. He was despised and rejected by others; a man of suffering and acquainted with infirmity; and as one from whom others hide their faces He was despised, and we held Him of no account" (NRSV).

Amazingly, Jesus was willing to deny Himself everything, even in the lowly way He came to us and even in His unattractive appearance. Jesus did not come as a regal and daunting king to overthrow the leaders of the day, but He arrived to be a humble

WHO CAN RESIST THE FACE OF PURE LOVE?

servant—to give up His life so that sin and death could be conquered. Yes, that is amazing.

But no matter how Jesus appeared, Mary would surely have loved that face no matter what. After all, who can resist the face of pure love?

Lord, I would seek Your face of love and follow You anywhere. Amen.

It Doesn't Amount to a Hill of Beans

Zealous? Yes. I ruthlessly pursued
and persecuted the church.
And when it comes to the righteousness
required by the law, my record
is spotless. But whatever I used to count
as my greatest accomplishments,
I've written them off as a loss because
of the Anointed One. And more so,
I now realize that all I gained and
thought was important was nothing
but yesterday's garbage compared
to knowing the Anointed Jesus
my Lord. For Him I have
thrown everything aside—
it's nothing but a pile of waste—
so that I may gain Him.

PHILIPPIANS 3:6–8 (VOICE)

Paul said it so well in Philippians, when he tells us that, because Christ has come, what he used to count as his great accomplishments—that is, persecuting the church—had to be written off as a loss.

What do we chase today with a passion that in the end won't amount to a hill of beans, as Mama says? The list could go on and on and on, right? But for each person that list could look very different. Some of our pursuits will get chucked later like rubbish, and some may reflect the lasting sheen of heavenly splendor. What do you think yours will look like?

SOME OF OUR PURSUITS WILL GET CHUCKED LATER LIKE RUBBISH, AND SOME MAY REFLECT THE LASTING SHEEN OF HEAVENLY SPLENDOR. WHAT DO YOU THINK YOURS WILL LOOK LIKE?

Father God, sometimes I get the feeling that I am chasing the wind in some of the things I choose to do with my life. I get a passion for all sorts of activities, but I am never sure if they are what You want me to do. Please guide me so that I might not waste my life but use it for Your purposes and Your glory. And in that, I know I will come to experience the peace and joy that I have always longed for. In Jesus' name I pray. Amen.

Fancy Seeing You Here!

On that same evening (Resurrection Sunday), the followers gathered together behind locked doors in fear that some of the Jewish leaders in Jerusalem were still searching for them. Out of nowhere, Jesus appeared in the center of the room.

Jesus: May each one of you be at peace.

As He was speaking, He revealed the wounds in His hands and side. The disciples began to celebrate as it sank in that they were really seeing the Lord.

JOHN 20:19–20 (VOICE)

Out of the blue, Beverly spotted her friend Sharlene at a special museum exhibit downtown. Bev scurried over to her friend and said, "Well, fancy meeting you here, my friend! I didn't know you were a fan of this artist. What fun." They hugged and squealed and cackled a bit as women sometimes do—and then they decided to stay together as they milled around the museum. They commented here and there. They strolled and sighed over the beauty of the art. Later, they lunched together. Their accidental meeting was considered a lovely serendipity.

Can you imagine that day when the disciples met in a room with locked doors—scared and confused—and then suddenly the resurrected Jesus appears, standing in front of them? I doubt the disciples replied with an ancient version of "Fancy seeing you here!" Instead there may have been a few seconds of stunned silence. Jesus offered them peace and showed them His hands and side. Then they must have broken out into quite a jubilant celebration. Jesus' appearance would, after all, change everything. It would alter life on planet earth forever. Nothing would or could be the same. Sin and death had been conquered. Love had won.

JESUS' APPEARANCE WOULD, AFTER ALL, CHANGE EVERYTHING.

In the end, Jesus' resurrection was and still is the greatest serendipity in the history of the world! Let us celebrate!

Dear Lord, thank You for sending Your Son to earth not only to live among us but to save us. I am eternally grateful to You. Amen.

Feeling Poorly

He heals the brokenhearted,
binding up their wounds.

PSALM 147:3 (TLB)

Come rain or shine, every Tuesday morning an older woman name Laverne would hobble along the dirt road toward the country store in order to buy her weekly groceries. She would push a tiny cart that had a tall red flag attached to it, so she could be seen easily along the road. A young man who was on his way to work always waved as he traveled by, and the older woman would yoo-hoo back at him.

Finally, the young man stopped and asked if she needed a ride, and Laverne replied that the walk helped to keep her healthy. But even then, the young man never took another route to work, because he liked to check on the older woman as he drove by, just to make sure she was okay. One day, he didn't see Laverne but only the little red flag. The older woman had taken a tumble and was lying in the ditch. The young man rushed to her side carrying the first aid kit from his car. He held her gently, while cleansing and binding her wounds. Tears streamed down Laverne's face, and he asked if he should take her to the hospital. "No,"

Laverne replied, "I am not crying out of pain, but from the kindness in your spirit."

Yes, sometimes people are feeling poorly. They might be injured in mind, body, or spirit. They may be suffering from a great loss or sorrow that overwhelms them. Or they might just be tired and world weary or they have stumbled and fallen. The Lord does help the brokenhearted. But as followers of Jesus and as Christians who want to emulate Him, then the Lord is most glad when we too become a comfort to the brokenhearted, and when we too bind up their wounds. Is there someone who needs to see that "kindness of spirit" from us today?

LAVERNE REPLIED, "I AM NOT CRYING OUT OF PAIN, BUT FROM THE KINDNESS IN YOUR SPIRIT."

Holy Spirit, please guide me. I want to be Your hands and heart to someone today. I am willing and able to help. Amen.

Your Face Is Gonna Freeze Like That!

*BE ANGRY [at sin—at immorality,
at injustice, at ungodly behavior],
YET DO NOT SIN; do not let your anger
[cause you shame, nor allow it to]
last until the sun goes down. And do
not give the devil an opportunity [to
lead you into sin by holding a grudge,
or nurturing anger, or harboring
resentment, or cultivating bitterness].*

EPHESIANS 4:26–27 (AMP)

So, your son, Byron, woke up on the wrong side of the bed, and at the breakfast table, even though he was chowing down on his very favorite treat, he made a face that looked as cute as a warthog. No, maybe it was more like a naked mole rat. Yeah, that one. Anyway, you suddenly caught yourself saying something your mother always said to you when you'd come down with a bad case of the uglies. You announced to Byron, "Your face is gonna freeze like that!" Then your son looked at you funny. Who knows what he thought about such an odd declaration, but it did make him laugh. Then all at once the mole rat morphed back into your dear sweet son again.

Face it (sorry about the pun), we all go ugly from time to time. And sometimes anger gets the best of us. Then when it festers day after day, the anger turns into bitterness. Once that settles in, you might as well give up on happiness. You're headed for what your mama might call "pure-o-dee misery!" Yes, taking that anger to bed might be the way of the world, but it's not the way of God.

OH, AND IF WE DO FEEL OBLIGED TO FREEZE AN EXPRESSION, MAYBE IT SHOULD BE A SMILE!

Are we going to get angry about stuff? No doubt about it. But the Lord wants us to give that anger to Him at the end of the day. Is that going to be an easy task? No. So, ask God for help. After all, the Lord won't ask us to do anything that He is not willing to help us with every step of the way.

Oh, and if we do feel obliged to freeze an expression, maybe it should be a smile!

Lord, teach me the beautiful art of letting my anger go at the end of the day. Amen.

As a mama myself, I have surely tried to know all things and do all things and be all things, but I am so grateful that people give me some grace. After all, I discovered long ago that I am not God. Only God can be God. And I am so fine with that!

Well, I Swanee!

Then Peter came to himself and said, "Now I know without a doubt that the Lord has sent His angel and rescued me from Herod's clutches and from everything the Jewish people were hoping would happen." When this had dawned on him, he went to the house of Mary the mother of John, also called Mark, where many people had gathered and were praying. Peter knocked at the outer entrance, and a servant named Rhoda came to answer the door. When she recognized Peter's voice, she was so overjoyed she ran back without opening it and exclaimed, "Peter is at the door!" "You're out of your mind," they told her.

ACTS 12:11–15 (NIV)

Lena enjoyed the company meetings, except for one thing: a woman named Cecily who liked to pretend she was Lena's supervisor even though she was an underling. That woman made hornets look like clueless tormentors. Yes, Cecily was the queen of little stinging harassments. Like interrupting Lena in a meeting. Or taking credit for her hard work. Or asking her for coffee. Or making her look like a fool in front of her boss. Oy!

So, after a few meltdowns at home, Lena decided to commit the woman and her malicious antics to some serious prayer. Lena did begin to notice some tiny changes, but then one day Cecily praised Lena in a meeting. And then offered to pass out the donuts and coffee. Lena sat flabbergasted, watching this sudden display of humility in Cecily. Lena caught herself murmuring what her granny always said when in utter astonishment, "Well, I swanee." Then two of the younger people sitting next to Lena wondered why she was mumbling about waterfowl.

WHEN WE'VE PRAYED AND THE MIRACLE ARRIVES, MAYBE WE SHOULD SKIP THE SHOCK AND GO STRAIGHT INTO CELEBRATION MODE!

In the book of Acts, when Rhoda delivered the news that Peter was knocking at the door after the group had just prayed for his miraculous release from prison, they said, "You're out of your mind." When we've prayed and the miracle arrives, maybe we should skip the shock and go straight into celebration mode!

Lord, please build my faith in You so that I can pray with a sense of expectation and hope! Amen.

If the Good Lord's Willing and the Creek Don't Rise

Do not allow this world to mold you in its own image. Instead, be transformed from the inside out by renewing your mind. As a result, you will be able to discern what God wills and whatever God finds good, pleasing, and complete.

ROMANS 12:2 (VOICE)

The word *tomorrow* sounds so hopeful, so filled with promise. The stuff of merry songs and happy thoughts. But tomorrow can also be riddled with one tiny word that dances precariously on the tip of a pin—if. That word can hold us up, change our course, or twist us into pieces if we let it. We humans make plans—impressive, detailed ones. If we're Christians, we pray over them too, but even as Christ-followers, we might allow that word "if" to undermine our good and godly agenda. What happened? Did Mama's old saying ring true, and this time it wasn't God's will? Did we not pray enough? Did we get too haughty or too faithless?

The book of Romans does give us some

direction concerning the will of God. First, we shouldn't get too cozy with the world's behaviors. Their modus operandi will trip us up, because sometimes people don't have our best interest at heart. But God does. We should allow the Lord to help us become new people by changing the way we reason and reflect. Then those future plans will come into being because we have been looking

THEN ALONG WITH OUR NEW WAY OF THINKING, THAT WORD "IF" WILL LOSE ITS HOLD ON US, AND OUR TOMORROWS WILL GET BACK THEIR HOPE AND PROMISE!

through God's eyes. Does that mean that life will now flow effortlessly? No, but it will help us discern the good and pleasing will of God. Then along with our new way of thinking, that word "if" will lose its hold on us, and our tomorrows will get back their hope and promise!

Lord Jesus, please transform my thinking and make me new. I truly want to do Your will. Amen.

Don't Get Smart with Me

*But He gives us more and more grace
[through the power of the Holy Spirit to
defy sin and live an obedient life that
reflects both our faith and our gratitude
for our salvation]. Therefore, it says,
"GOD IS OPPOSED TO THE PROUD AND
HAUGHTY, but [continually] gives [the
gift of] GRACE TO THE HUMBLE [who
turn away from self-righteousness]."*

JAMES 4:6 (AMP)

When kids get kind of sassy, sometimes a mama might say, "Don't get smart with me!" But adults can get disrespectful at times too. In front of each other and even before God. Usually that kind of 'tude means that there's a bit of pride sneaking around in one's spirit. Or maybe parading around for all to see! In recent years pride has attempted to adorn itself with acceptability and even modern sophistication. The world says we're supposed to not only feel pride but flaunt it and celebrate it. Really?

In James, it states the opposite—that God sets Himself against those who are haughty. And then it goes on to say that there is grace for those who are humble. Okay, grace sounds lovely. Several verses down in James 4:10, it reads, "Humble yourselves before the Lord, and he will exalt you" (ESV). Hmm. Okay, but realistically, if we are exalted, won't we be right back playing tiddlywinks with pride again? That sounds like a real paradox. The difference is, if we have obeyed God by humbling ourselves, He will in turn lift us up as a reward. Does that mean we can then indulge in a big splurge of pride—you know, like gobbling up a pint of double fudge ice cream after a diet? No, but it does mean we can thank God for promoting and praising us, and we can delight in His blessing!

> LORD JESUS, IF YOU CHOOSE TO EXALT ME, REMIND ME ALWAYS THAT YOU ARE THE SOURCE OF ALL MY BLESSINGS!

Lord Jesus, please give me grace for the journey. I want to be Your useable and humble servant. Then if You choose to exalt me, remind me always that You are the source of all my blessings! Thank You for every gift, both great and small. Amen.

Making a Mountain Out of a Molehill

That is why I tell you not to worry about everyday life—whether you have enough food and drink, or enough clothes to wear. Isn't life more than food, and your body more than clothing? Look at the birds. They don't plant or harvest or store food in barns, for your heavenly Father feeds them. And aren't you far more valuable to Him than they are? Can all your worries add a single moment to your life?

MATTHEW 6:25–27 (NLT)

Life is full of stubby little molehills that we inflate into mountains, right? We bang our spiritual toes on them by worrying and obsessing and giving in to catastrophic thinking. We become masters at the fine art of fretting! Except none of it is artsy *or* fine. We blow things out of proportion like, "Right during the meeting, I spilled my coffee all over my boss's suit. Oh man, my blunder was epic. Shoot me now!" Or, "What did my friend really mean by that brief text? She must be angry at me. Maybe she doesn't even want to be friends anymore." Or, "My family rarely calls me, and they don't say they love me unless I say it first. I must have been a bad parent. I feel unloved and worthless. I don't know why I still hang onto this life."

But sometimes life really does plop a mountain of a problem smack dab in our path. For instance, all three scenarios could indeed escalate from imagining the worst to becoming the worst. People do get fired. Friends abandon friends. And sometimes adult children don't

> WE BECOME MASTERS AT THE FINE ART OF FRETTING! EXCEPT NONE OF IT IS ARTSY *OR* FINE.

care for their parents as they should. But the Lord still wants us to pray and trust Him rather than worry. Sound too good to be true or too hard to pull off? Maybe, but God has proven Himself to be worthy of our trust. Does He always swoop in like a superhero and fix life as we request? No. But the Lord is there, ever working for our good. Embrace the promises of God. He will make good on them . . .

Lord, show me how to trust You with the molehills and the mountains! Amen.

Early to Bed and Early to Rise Makes You Healthy, Wealthy, and Wise

Lazy people want much but get little,
while the diligent are prospering.

PROVERBS 13:4 (TLB)

Truth be told, Geraldine had a love affair with the couch. She discovered to her delight that she could conduct most of her life from that very spot. She could eat there—no real need for a kitchen table. She could sleep there, lounge, splay herself out like a lazy cat, play with her cell phone for hours, do a movie marathon, lounge some more. Hey, lounging had its benefits! And for some astonishing reason, the more Geraldine goofed off, the more other people tended to do stuff for her. What a deal. Of course, sometimes they had a bad attitude about endlessly helping her with everything. Imagine! Why would they feel taken advantaged of? After all, she had big dreams.

But somewhere down the pike, Geraldine realized that she had gotten unhealthy just sitting there, not to mention sluggish in her mind and, well, miserable. And the worst part was that she no longer felt close to God. Then later when Geraldine checked her bank account—it was empty. For a while, she got angry. After all, her friends were already meeting many of their life goals. She deserved the same blessings. Didn't she?

Proverbs 13:4 says it perfectly. Great life advice. Maybe that's why Mama always said, "Early to bed and early to rise makes you healthy, wealthy, and wise." Of course, Geraldine's mama was hoping her daughter would rise early from bed so that she could actually go to work!

Eventually Geraldine looked in the mirror, and the mirror couldn't lie—she had become a rat-haired sloth. Perhaps it was time to get a job. Then somewhere in the heavenly realms, Geraldine's mother thought she might have heard the sound of angels rejoicing!

EVENTUALLY GERALDINE LOOKED IN THE MIRROR, AND THE MIRROR COULDN'T LIE—SHE HAD BECOME A RAT-HAIRED SLOTH!

Lord, help me to find a balance between being a workaholic and being lazy. I want to be all that You created me to be. Amen.

Gimme Some Sugar

*When the angels had left them
and gone into heaven, the shepherds
said to one another, "Let's go to
Bethlehem and see this thing that has
happened, which the Lord has told us
about." So they hurried off and found
Mary and Joseph, and the baby,
who was lying in the manger.
When they had seen Him,
they spread the word concerning what
had been told them about this child,
and all who heard it were amazed at
what the shepherds said to them.*

LUKE 2:15–18 (NIV)

It's early Christmas morning, and the kids are already jumping on your bed. Bleary-eyed, you could sure use a caffeine jumpstart, but hey, it's one of the best days of the year, so you rise and shine. Soon the family is gathered round the tree, and everybody is ripping and tearing and laughing and giving each other plenty of sugar. Wonderful stuff. Can't you imagine that the celestial beings hovering nearby might fall into curious wonder too? Yes, the Christmas gift exchange is one of the sweetest moments of the year—not the processed sugary kind that fills the stomach, but the spirit kind that fills the heart.

The best gifts ever given to mankind, though, are from God. They are Christmas and Easter. The redemption God gave us through Christ makes for glorious celebrations. And because we are so grateful, what can we give back to God? Mark 12:30 says, "Love the Lord your God with all your heart and with all your soul and with all your mind and with all your strength" (NIV).

YES, MAY WE MAKE JESUS PART OF OUR FAMILY AS WE GATHER ROUND . . .

That would add even more warmth and sweetness to the Christmas gift exchange. After all, God delights in us. He wants not only to redeem us, but to be with us and love us—and to be loved by us. Yes, may we make Jesus part of our family as we gather round . . .

Lord, we give You a place of honor in our family, not just on Christmas and Easter, but every day of the year! Amen.

Pretty Is as Pretty Does

Never tire of loyalty and kindness.
Hold these virtues tightly.
Write them deep within your heart.

PROVERBS 3:3 (TLB)

The older couple walked along the almost deserted beach, watching the changing colors of the setting sun against the gentle rise and fall of the undulating waves. The couple sighed, grateful that the earth still held some beauty for them. When they picked up a small object that had washed up on shore, they were curious as to what it was. They turned the faceted object over and over in their hands. The sun lit each and every facet, making the mysterious gift twinkle and glisten like a jewel. Little by little a tender "knowing" seeped into their spirits. The moment they realized what it was—the gift of kindness–they wept with joy, for the world had forgotten that such a treasure could be so easily found.

Then not far away, a young woman made her way down the same beach, looking forlorn and alone. The couple decided to give her the treasure. The young woman accepted this gift of kindness, awakened into joy, and went on her way with a lighter step. The older couple smiled and then laughed, for they too had not felt so light in years. As the older couple strolled toward home, now hand in hand, they wrote the virtue of kindness deep within their hearts. They would never forget such a precious gift, and they knew each time it was passed on, the world would begin to remember . . .

AS THE OLDER COUPLE STROLLED TOWARD HOME, NOW HAND IN HAND, THEY WROTE THE VIRTUE OF KINDNESS DEEP WITHIN THEIR HEARTS.

Heavenly Father, in our hectic and busy world, we are forgetting about the importance of kindness. Please help me to remember to be generous when giving this beautiful and precious God-gift. In Jesus' holy name I pray. Amen.

Barking Up the Wrong Tree

Do not love the world or the things in the world. If anyone loves the world, the love of the Father is not in him. For all that is in the world—the desires of the flesh and the desires of the eyes and pride of life—is not from the Father but is from the world. And the world is passing away along with its desires, but whoever does the will of God abides forever.

I JOHN 2:15–17 (ESV)

The world is like a big steel locomotive chugging and barreling along a windswept landscape. Now envision one of those little toy train sets you give your child at Christmastime. You know, the one that makes the little choo-choo noises as it moves along a tiny track? Well, that is us. We don't stand a chance against that locomotive—at least not on our own.

Most folks like to travel along with the crowd. They yearn to be accepted and to be part of a club or gang or guild or league or alliance, or anything really. Yes, those desires for inclusion and belonging are so powerful sometimes that they override the discernment we gain as we mature in Christ, and sometimes they even defy our basic common sense!

If the way of the world were good and godly, well, we might want to get on board that big powerful train and ride the ride! But sometimes the world can give us a dangerous traveling experience. In fact, your mama might say, "Honey, if you want to follow Christ, then trying to follow the ways of the world is surely barking up the wrong tree!"

GOD'S WAYS ARE NOT OUR WAYS, AND THAT IS A VERY GOOD THING BECAUSE OUR WAYS HAVEN'T WORKED SINCE THE GARDEN OF EDEN!

What to do?

You can flee from anything that doesn't line up with Scripture. Go with God. Rest in Him. Follow His lead. God's ways are not our ways, and that is a very good thing because our ways haven't worked since the Garden of Eden!

O Lord, too many times I have desired the things of this world far above You. Help me to remember that this world will someday pass away. But You are forever! Amen.

Thoughts
FROM MAMA
by Anita Higman

Being a mama, I have sung a thousand lullabies through the years. I may have been off-key and I may not have known all the words, but I tried to sing to my babies with such heart and such love that sometimes I could almost hear the angels humming along.

You Are the Best Thing since Sliced Bread

*Therefore, if anyone is in Christ,
he is a new creation. The old has passed
away; behold, the new has come.
All this is from God, who through Christ
reconciled us to himself and gave us
the ministry of reconciliation.*

II CORINTHIANS 5:17–18 (ESV)

The woman stood on the sidewalk, staring in through the bakery window. She intended to sneak a look at that newfangled contraption people were talking about. Hmm. Should she go in and give it a chance or continue to just gawk with curiosity? Would her friends scoff at her? Finally, the woman reached for the door handle, boldly strode up to the counter, and ordered a loaf of pre-sliced bread!

Yes, when the first bakery provided pre-sliced bread, it became a big hit right away. Ahhh, yes, just wonderful. And, well, that is how Mama sees you. You're a big hit in her mind too, and she is always ready to celebrate family.

God loves His family too. John 3:16 reminds us, "For God so loved the world that He gave His one and only Son, that whoever believes in Him shall not perish but have eternal life" (NIV). Yes, through Christ's redemption we are made new, and we are reconciled to God. It is almost too much to take in—this unfathomable love and attention. And it is so much better than sliced bread!

MAY WE NOT MERELY GAZE AT HEAVEN'S OFFER OF GRACE WITH CURIOSITY, BUT INSTEAD PARTAKE BOLDLY OF REDEMPTION. THEN LET THE FAMILY CELEBRATION BEGIN!

May we not merely gaze at heaven's offer of grace with curiosity, but instead partake boldly of redemption. Then let the family celebration begin!

Dear Father God, thank You for loving me so deeply that You wanted me to be reconciled to You. Thank You for sending Your Son to die for me, so that I might be offered forgiveness for my sins. I love You dearly. Help me to love You more every day! In Jesus' holy name I pray. Amen.

You Would Argue with a Fence Post

Run away from infantile indulgence. Run after mature righteousness—faith, love, peace—joining those who are in honest and serious prayer before God. Refuse to get involved in inane discussions; they always end up in fights. God's servant must not be argumentative, but a gentle listener and a teacher who keeps cool, working firmly but patiently with those who refuse to obey. You never know how or when God might sober them up with a change of heart and a turning to the truth, enabling them to escape the Devil's trap, where they are caught and held captive, forced to run his errands.

II TIMOTHY 2:23–26
(THE MESSAGE)

As a courtesy, you said you'd watch your neighbor's cat for her, but once the woman's darling pet made herself at home in your house, you realized you'd agreed to guard some sort of furball fiend! You were standing there, minding your own business, when the cat decided to give you a snarl and a scratch just because she didn't like your condescending expression! Right then you decide that your pet-sitting days were officially over.

Have you ever been around someone who acts a little like that cat? Perhaps it's a male coworker who seems to thrive on ruffling up feathers and dragging people into inane discussions that end in an angry brouhaha. In other words, he would argue with a fencepost! Ecclesiastes 7:9 expresses the problem of angry and argumentative people with humorous clarity. "Don't be quick to fly off the handle. Anger boomerangs. You can spot a fool by the lumps on his head" (THE MESSAGE). May we limit the number of lumps on our heads by not quarreling and by not allowing ourselves to be enticed into arguments!

> DON'T BE QUICK TO FLY OFF THE HANDLE. ANGER BOOMERANGS. YOU CAN SPOT A FOOL BY THE LUMPS ON HIS HEAD (ECCLESIASTES 7:9 THE MESSAGE).

Lord, help me to avoid getting pulled into spats and squabbles that don't turn out to be helpful or healing. Amen.

You Are the Spitting Image of Your Mama!

So God created humankind in His image, in the image of God He created them; male and female He created them.

GENESIS 1:27 (NRSV)

Mama may not shout, "Child, you are the spitting image of me," but she sure will love it if that big announcement comes from anybody else. And preferably broadcasted to a very large audience! After all, a mama relishes the idea of her child looking like her. Why wouldn't she? Mamas love their babies, and kids are little reflections of their parents. Of course, generally, children have their own facades, but we can usually see glimmers of us here and there. Maybe a similar perky nose or rosebud lips or a shock of wild hair. But then sometimes a child might look exactly like her mom or dad, and that is always amazing to see!

On a more heavenly note, the Bible says in Genesis that we are made in the image of God. Hard to imagine, but it's true. How do we handle that glorious truth? Do we believe it? Celebrate the news? Share it with others? From the viewpoint of the parent, do we make God proud by reflecting His radiance? Do people see glimmers of Him in us—God's love and beauty, His joy, peace, and wonder? Hopefully, with every passing day—as we mature as Christians—we are becoming more and more like our Father-God.

DO PEOPLE SEE GLIMMERS OF HIM IN US—GOD'S LOVE AND BEAUTY, HIS JOY, PEACE, AND WONDER? HOPEFULLY, WITH EVERY PASSING DAY, WE ARE BECOMING MORE AND MORE LIKE OUR FATHER-GOD.

Are you a chip off the ol' masterpiece?

Dear God, I want to make You proud in all I do. I willingly accept Your divine disciplines to make me more like You every day. I would rather receive Your holy corrections than accept countless praises from the enemy. Lord, I want to reflect You so well in this fallen and hurting world that people will know right away Who I belong to—You! In Jesus' holy name I pray. Amen.

Because I Said So, That's Why!

God spoke all these words: "I am the LORD your God, who brought you out of Egypt, out of the land of slavery. You shall have no other gods before Me."

EXODUS 20:1–3 (NIV)

Our wee ones can be so cute. They laugh with abandon. They rush up to you with bunches of wildflowers. They make sweet declarations of love. Ahh, yes, they can bring a virtual lovefest into your heart and home.

BUT—just as your children can warm you all over, they can break your heart just as easily. Julie can grab a toy out of the hand of her sibling just to enjoy the inevitable red-faced wail. Bobby can wrench his tiny hand from yours and disobediently run away into a busy street. Then as your kids grow up, they may take their rebellion to much more defiant and dangerous levels. And they may no longer respond when dear mama says, "Do it because I said so."

Within the plethora of godly advice in the Bible, God gave mankind the Ten Commandments to make sure we lived a life of joy and not of hurt. But today, how many people know all these divine instructions or actually follow them?

We get the notion that these rules are meant to punish us or to ruin our fun. Not true. God's precepts are meant to give us divine parameters—to keep us safe from straying beyond the barbwire fences of life where landmines abound. Makes one shudder to think of it!

May our souls long for innocent days. May we no longer choose to go our own frightful ways, but to instead humbly stroll through the meadows with God. We may even want to pick a bunch of wildflowers and shout, "I love You, God!"

MAY WE HUMBLY STROLL THROUGH THE MEADOWS WITH GOD. WE MAY EVEN WANT TO PICK A BUNCH OF WILDFLOWERS AND SHOUT, "I LOVE YOU, GOD!"

Lord, I choose You and Your ways all the days of my life! Amen.

More Than You Can Shake a Stick At

You spread out a table before me,
provisions in the midst of attack from
my enemies; You care for all my needs,
anointing my head with soothing,
fragrant oil, filling my cup again and
again with Your grace.

PSALM 23:5 (VOICE)

There's nothing like sitting down in your favorite café with your best friend and having the server swing by to give you yet another refill of their finest French roast coffee. The steam rises. You breathe deeply of the aroma. Your hands embrace the mug. You sigh. Yes, you're swooning in the wonderful mix of comfortable ambiance, friendly fellowship, and intoxicating brew. You can now sense hope on the horizon! Life is good. That's why you keep going back. The experience has "abundance" written all over it. Or as your mama might say, "More than you can shake a stick at!"

When it comes to cup after cup after cup of blessing, God outdoes everybody. Hands down. When He sends gifts, they are sublime. He blesses our earth with sunshine and rain and bountiful harvests. He gives mankind the knowledge to create articles of usefulness and wonder. Everywhere in nature we see God's over-the-top masterpieces. From the lacy enchantment of snowflakes to the spectacular mountains that leave us breathless, His Creation is an awesome and abundant gift!

WHEN IT COMES TO CUP AFTER CUP AFTER CUP OF BLESSING, GOD OUTDOES EVERYBODY. HANDS DOWN. WHEN HE SENDS GIFTS, THEY ARE SUBLIME.

God also makes our cup overflow with mercies, with love that is eternal and grace through Christ's gift. Abundance indeed.

Almighty God, I don't think I ever thank You enough for all Your blessings that You pour into my life. My cup overflows, and I am truly awed by Your majesty and Your generosity and Your beautiful transforming love. My soul bursts with gratitude. In Jesus' holy name I pray. Amen.

If All Your Friends Jumped Off a Cliff, Would You Jump Too?

Do not be deceived: "Bad company corrupts good morals." Be sober-minded [be sensible, wake up from your spiritual stupor] as you ought, and stop sinning; for some [of you] have no knowledge of God [you are disgracefully ignorant of Him, and ignore His truths]. I say this to your shame.

I CORINTHIANS 15:33–34 (AMP)

Yeah, she's been your friend since forever—bosom buddies like Anne of Green Gables and Diana—but over the last few years she's not been herself. Your friend used to be a guileless Jesus-follower, but lately she seems to follow anything and everything that pleases her.

On a pricklier note, you think maybe she's become bad company, but you're not sure. How in the world can you tell? Shouldn't there be warning signs? Indeed.

Have you noticed that in order to keep the peace with your friend you've had to make a few compromises? Maybe you've gone to some places with her that you wouldn't normally go—places that make you feel uncomfortable in your spirit. Have you romanced some beliefs that you know are not right biblically? Or perhaps you've started to read some of her favorite literature that steers you toward trusting in yourself and away from loving the Lord.

Yes, if you have a friend who is about to jump off a cliff spiritually, tell her of the danger, but if she is defiant and is intent on convincing you to head over the cliff with her, shake your hand loose and flee. Pray for your friend always, but God tells us clearly that bad company corrupts good morals. Proverbs 12:26 reminds us succinctly, "The righteous choose their friends carefully, but the way of the wicked leads them astray" (NIV).

The Lord is good to us, and if we ask, He will graciously give us those guileless, loving relationships that remind us of the heartwarming friendships of days gone by.

THE LORD IS GOOD TO US, AND IF WE ASK, HE WILL GRACIOUSLY GIVE US THOSE GUILELESS, LOVING RELATIONSHIPS THAT REMIND US OF THE HEARTWARMING FRIENDSHIPS OF DAYS GONE BY.

Holy Spirit, give me wisdom as I choose my friends. Amen.

It's Blowing Up a Storm

We are pressed on every side by troubles, but not crushed and broken. We are perplexed because we don't know why things happen as they do, but we don't give up and quit. We are hunted down, but God never abandons us. We get knocked down, but we get up again and keep going.

II CORINTHIANS 4:8–9 (TLB)

The clouds darken and boil just beyond the hills. The distant thunder rolls closer and rumbles as if the sky is hungry and angry. The wind blusters in, gusting downward in whooshing shafts of air that nearly suck the breath out of you. That billowing gale is coming your way, and the scene makes you remember your mama hollering to you when you were a kid, "Come on in now. It's blowing up a storm!" Maybe you stayed outside in the storm awhile longer, to feel the power of it or just to get your mother's ire up. Or maybe it was because you liked knowing your mama was going to keep hollering—that it proved her affection for you and gave you the certainty of love.

Life will indeed be riddled with storms. Some little squalls. Some dark and angry storms with hidden cyclones that nearly take your breath away. We can be grateful that even if we get battered and knocked down by these storms, God will help us back up. We can know that the God who called the cosmos into existence is the same

MAY WE ACKNOWLEDGE GOD'S PRESENCE. EMBRACE HIS AFFECTIONATE OVERTURES. AND ALWAYS KNOW DEEP DOWN THAT SWEET CERTAINTY OF HIS DIVINE LOVE.

God who calls you by name and is our help in times of great trouble.

May we acknowledge God's presence. Embrace His affectionate overtures. And always know deep down that sweet certainty of His divine love.

Lord God, there seems to be some kind of storm brewing in my life almost daily. Please be ever near me. I am helpless without Your divine guidance and strength. In Jesus' name I pray. Amen.

Don't Get Your Feathers Ruffled!

Everyone will share the story of Your wonderful goodness; they will sing with joy about Your righteousness.
The LORD is merciful and compassionate, slow to get angry and filled with unfailing love.
The LORD is good to everyone. He showers compassion on all His creation.

PSALM 145:7–9 (NLT)

If you have ever seen a geyser blow, then you know—it is quite a memorable sight. And during that spewing eruption, the spectacle may remind you of someone you know who has a cantankerous constitution. Yeah, everybody knows somebody like that, eh? At work, maybe in your family, your child's playgroup, a friend or two, a checker at the grocery store, or it could even be someone at church. Or maybe it's you! When that person gets enraged over something, well, she might get quiet and red-faced for a moment, but then step back—yep, she's going to blow!

The earth has plenty of those boiling-cauldron style temperaments, which doesn't make for a lot of goodwill toward men.

But we can be assured and made more peace-filled to remember that God isn't like that. The Lord is slow to anger. He does not have the frail and fallen nature of humanity, which is riddled with self-interest and poor judgment. God instead shows us love that is steadfast and everlasting. In fact, the Lord showers kindness on all that He has created—including me and you.

> MAY WE ALLOW THE HOLY SPIRIT TO FLOOD OUR SPIRITS WITH HIS GOODNESS, SO THAT IF PEOPLE DO FIND US GUSHING, IT WILL BE WITH GOD'S RADIANT LIGHT!

When we do get our feathers ruffled—as Mama might say—may we crowd out those ireful outbursts with praise to God. May we tell of His goodness and mercy. May we allow the Holy Spirit to flood our spirits with His goodness, so that if people do find us gushing, it will be with God's radiant light!

Dearest Jesus, You know that from time to time I let my temper get the best of me. Please flood my soul with Your patience and mercy, Your goodness and light! Amen.

I like big chuckles, big
cheering, and big love,
because I am a mama.
I take pleasure in big
food, big holidays, and
big appetites. But in the
midst of my big giving, I
sure wouldn't mind a big
hug coming from you!

A Watched Pot Never Boils

As a prisoner of the Lord, I urge you:
Live a life that is worthy of the calling
He has graciously extended to you.
Be humble. Be gentle. Be patient.
Tolerate one another in an atmosphere
thick with love.

EPHESIANS 4:1–2 (VOICE)

Bev maneuvered over to the faster lane, finessing her way through traffic. She prided herself in the fact that she also had speedier and smarter ways to work, pay bills, clean, cook, and organize pretty much everything. If Bev had a pot ready to boil, she might check it a dozen times. Much to Bev's chagrin, the silly thing never seemed to come to a boil! The problem was in all her multitasking, manipulating mania—that is, trying to make the absolute most of every minute—Bev had forgotten how to live. How to love, to be gentle, patient, and humble. Unfortunately, Bev had worked the hardest at making herself into a miserable woman!

One day, when Bev had reached the peak of her impatience but the end of her happiness, she decided to ask God for help. She wondered what would happen next, because she knew when she asked God to help her mature as a Christian, it was a prayer He seemed to delight in answering. Soon Bev was invited to rest instead of run, and while that went against all her instincts, she was able to enjoy life with patience.

PERHAPS EVERYONE, YOUNG AND OLD, COULD BENEFIT FROM THE QUIET ART OF PATIENCE.

Perhaps everyone, young and old, could benefit from the quiet art of patience.

O Lord, I know I am notorious for being impatient and pushy and anything but gentle and humble. I am truly sorry for my insensitivity and disobedience, and I humbly ask You for Your forgiveness. Please help me to grow up into a mature Christian woman. I want to be more like You every day so that I might glorify You and be usable in Your kingdom. Amen.

Bless Your Pea-Picking Heart

Fear not, little flock,
for it is your Father's good pleasure
to give you the kingdom.

LUKE 12:32 (ESV)

In olden times, down South you may have heard someone say, "Bless your pea-picking heart." It can be used as a sweet form of endearment, and it does indeed have a pleasant sort of downhome ring to it. Sort of makes you want to play a game of checkers, or bake a basket of biscuits to take over to your neighbor's house for a gift, or maybe even learn to play a merry tune on a banjo!

Ah yes, endearments. We love them, don't we? They make us feel set apart, beloved, and anything but ordinary. Did you know that God does the same thing for us, by giving us a treasured nickname? In Luke we are referred to as "little flock."

To know we are deeply loved by God can make us slow our frantic pace, calm our hearts, and allow our smile to return. We can laugh brighter, love bigger, and live life with all our hearts, knowing love is here in the name of Jesus. First John 4:19 says, "So you see, our love for Him comes as a result of His loving us first" (TLB).

God loved us first—with great passion of the heart. An epic love story is being played out, and we are at the center of it!

GOD LOVED US FIRST—WITH GREAT PASSION OF THE HEART. AN EPIC LOVE STORY IS BEING PLAYED OUT, AND WE ARE AT THE CENTER OF IT!

Dearest Father, my heart overflows with such gratitude to know how much You love me. This fallen world can be a difficult place to live, but knowing of Your affection, and attention, and devotion makes life not only bearable but beautiful. I love You dearly, Lord! In Jesus' holy name I pray. Amen.

Mama Didn't Raise No Fool

An empty-head thinks mischief is fun,
but a mindful person relishes wisdom.

PROVERBS 10:23 (THE MESSAGE)

Okay, on Halloween night, some of the local teen guys decided to load an old outhouse on a truck and situate it smack dab in the middle of Main Street in the small town. The next morning, the prank made a lot of people laugh. And the old farmer—who had a sense of humor—kind of chuckled too. But then nobody seemed to want to help the farmer put the outhouse back, and so he injured his back trying to wrestle the tiny building onto his pickup. The boys never apologized, and they never bothered to think much about the old man again, except to be proud every time they told their outhouse tale.

Well, Mama tried not to raise any fools, but we all have foolish tendencies. We all have from time to time done things that seemed like empty-headed tomfoolery—even as adults. It just may not be dragging outhouses into the middle of town on Halloween. But people can be very creative when it comes to pranks and trouble-making mischief.

The good Lord is willing and ready to help

us trade in our tricks for the godly treats of understanding and good sense. James 1:5 tells us, "If any of you lacks wisdom [to guide him through

WELL, MAMA TRIED NOT TO RAISE ANY FOOLS, BUT WE ALL HAVE FOOLISH TENDENCIES.

a decision or circumstance], he is to ask of [our benevolent] God, who gives to everyone generously and without rebuke or blame, and it will be given to him" (AMP).

Holy Spirit, please guide me into wisdom and away from my own foolish ways. I want to always do what is right, but sometimes I still get myself into trouble. Help me to cling to You and Your divine ways all the days of my life. Amen.

If Mama Ain't Happy, Ain't Nobody Happy

Live creatively, friends. If someone falls into sin, forgivingly restore him, saving your critical comments for yourself. You might be needing forgiveness before the day's out. Stoop down and reach out to those who are oppressed. Share their burdens, and so complete Christ's law. If you think you are too good for that, you are badly deceived.

GALATIANS 6:2–3 (THE MESSAGE)

There's nobody on earth quite like a mama. No siree. She totes, cooks, cleans, hugs, doctors, cheers, plans, shares, chauffeurs, encourages, plays, and loves.

But then sometimes poor Mama might come undone. You know, she might deflate like a popped birthday balloon lying flat on the floor, looking spent and sad. Why so? Maybe someone forgot to help and support Mama. Someone forgot to carry her burden. We all need to carry each other's burdens. Not just Mama's. Sounds good, but what does that look like on a practical level? One example might be to give the simple gift of listening. Not the kind that nods and glances at the clock, but the kind that really takes in what is being said. Other examples are hugs and smiles and praises. These only take a moment, and yet they can make all the difference—between someone being disheartened and someone being gladdened.

When we make others happy, it will please God. After all, Christ came as a servant, and we are to follow His example. And when we give of ourselves and share other's burdens in the name of Christ, there is a sacred beauty to it that will in turn warm, uplift, and lighten our own souls.

WHEN WE GIVE OF OURSELVES AND SHARE OTHER'S BURDENS IN THE NAME OF CHRIST, THERE IS A SACRED BEAUTY TO IT THAT WILL IN TURN WARM, UPLIFT, AND LIGHTEN OUR OWN SOULS.

Lord God, sometimes I get so busy I forget that many people around me are hurting. Give me compassion for others and help me to have the heart of a servant. In Jesus' name I pray. Amen.

Running Around Like a Chicken with Its Head Cut Off!

*And He got up and [sternly] rebuked
the wind and said to the sea,
"Hush, be still (muzzled)!"
And the wind died down
[as if it had grown weary] and
there was [at once] a great calm
[a perfect peacefulness].*

MARK 4:39 (AMP)

We humans are quite skilled at busyness. In fact, if we're not busy we just pretend to be busy. We run around twitching like a chicken who's had his head, well, let's not go there. Anyway, here's one scenario...

Clair decided to make a pie for the church bizarre, even though the church had plenty of pies. But still, she raced to the store, sped home, and proceeded to make a homemade pie. Then as she sliced the apples too quickly, she sliced her finger and had to get a bandage. Good grief, she was out of bandages, so she zoomed back to the store. But Clair had been in such a rush, she'd forgotten to check the gas tank. Empty. Stopped. Game over. There on the road with her empty gas tank, her butchered finger, and an unmade pie, Clair cried, wondering why she lived such a frantic life.

Maybe to avoid beating ourselves to pieces, some wise questions might be, "Is what I'm doing really necessary, or am I making myself ill with busywork? Do I really need to say yes to every request I receive, even if it's church related? Why do I feel guilty whenever I take a much-needed rest?"

THE LORD IS MAKER OF ALL, AND HE CAN NOT ONLY CREATE THE MIGHTY SEAS, BUT HE CAN CALM THEM. AND THE GOOD LORD CAN QUIET US DOWN TOO. SHALL WE NOT LET HIM CREATE A HOLY HUSH DOWN DEEP IN OUR SOULS?

The Lord is maker of all, and He can not only create the mighty seas, but He can calm them. And the good Lord can quiet us down too. Shall we not let Him create a holy hush down deep in our souls?

Jesus, give me the wisdom to know when to work and when to rest. Amen.

Just Wait Until Your Daddy Gets Home!

My son, do not despise the Lord's discipline or be weary of his reproof, for the Lord reproves him whom he loves, as a father the son in whom he delights.

PROVERBS 3:11–12 (ESV)

As adults, you may recall various reprimands handed out by your mom or dad while you were growing up. And then there might have been times when your mom was so tired or upset that she said the famous line—"Just wait until your daddy gets home!"—to allow her husband to divvy out the reprimands. But whoever dealt out the corrections most likely wasn't met with a "Thanks, Mom and Dad, for the discipline. I sure needed that!"

Unlikely. And yet all good parents should correct their children from time to time. If they don't, there is no real love. How would it come off if your child did something truly awful or dangerous and you just shrugged and walked away? That kind of reaction would eventually confuse and frighten a child much worse than a chastisement.

So, since God is the greatest parent of all, He too corrects His children in a way that is loving and effective. Proverbs 12:1 intensifies the language even further by bluntly saying, "Whoever loves discipline loves knowledge, but whoever hates correction is stupid" (NIV). Think of all the times we've tried to escape from the Lord's discipline. Perhaps we are each like an angry bear cub who's gotten itself entangled in a briar patch, but we end up growling and pawing at the man who is trying to set us free! The good news is that God has a long-suffering kind of attitude with us. He loves us. In fact, He absolutely delights in each of us!

PERHAPS WE ARE EACH LIKE AN ANGRY BEAR CUB WHO'S GOTTEN ITSELF ENTANGLED IN A BRIAR PATCH, BUT WE END UP GROWLING AND PAWING AT THE MAN WHO IS TRYING TO SET US FREE!

Lord, teach me not to loathe but love Your discipline! Amen.

Did You Just Fall Off the Turnip Truck?

Finally, brothers and sisters,
fill your minds with beauty and truth.
Meditate on whatever is honorable,
whatever is right, whatever is pure,
whatever is lovely, whatever is good,
whatever is virtuous and praiseworthy.

PHILIPPIANS 4:8 (VOICE)

When we recall the old saying about falling off the turnip truck, we might conjure up images of Elly May Clampett from *The Beverly Hillbillies* riding into the city in that old dilapidated jalopy. She seemed so full of life, so simple and trusting and naïve, and refreshingly unfamiliar with the wily and overly savvy ways of city dwellers. Our society tends to be unsettled by people who are innocent and who might have a guileless way about them. Many times, when people come across purity, the first thing they want to do is take some of it away or taint it, rather than emulate that beautiful quality or cheer it on.

But God's ways are different, and He would be pleased for us to think on things that are pure and good and virtuous—and things that are lovely and truthful and noble. The good Lord not only wants those divine qualities to be meditated on, but He would like those qualities to so permeate our souls that they are lived out in our daily comings and goings.

To be a Christ-follower, we don't need to be a caricature of naivete with a big goofy grin. But we should always be winsome and wise, and filled with His good grace.

TO BE A CHRIST-FOLLOWER, WE DON'T NEED TO BE A CARICATURE OF NAIVETE WITH A BIG GOOFY GRIN. BUT WE SHOULD ALWAYS BE WINSOME AND WISE, AND FILLED WITH HIS GOOD GRACE.

Dear Lord, sometimes I feel the world wants me to be very different from how You created me to be. I get mixed messages from people, and it causes me confusion and stress. Please give me wisdom in the way I should think and the courage to live it out daily! Amen.

How Do You Know You Don't Like It If You Haven't Tasted It?

But the serpent said to the woman, "You will not surely die. For God knows that when you eat of it your eyes will be opened, and you will be like God, knowing good and evil." So when the woman saw that the tree was good for food, and that it was a delight to the eyes, and that the tree was to be desired to make one wise, she took of its fruit and ate, and she also gave some to her husband who was with her, and he ate.

GENESIS 3:4–6 (ESV)

Most of us have heard the old saying from Mama, "How do you know you don't like it if you haven't tried it?" The phrase is meant to teach kids that it's good to try new foods, even if they look green and icky. Yep, Mama will try most anything to coax her kids into eating right.

In the Garden of Eden, there was a lot of "convincing" going on, but it was of the evil kind. We are never told how long it took for the serpent to persuade Eve to eat of the forbidden fruit. The serpent may have tried for a very long time, and he may have used every argument imaginable to coerce them both into sin. What we do know is that Adam and Eve chose not to trust God. The first couple had every joy at their fingertips as well as romantic love. And if that wasn't enough, they had the unfathomable pleasure of strolling in the cool of the evening with their God. They had everything, and they gave it all away for a chance at something more. Something good they thought God was withholding from them. That was a lie most wicked.

GOD WITHHOLDS NO GOOD THING FROM YOU. HE HAS YOUR BEST INTEREST AT HEART, NOW, TOMORROW, AND FOREVERMORE.

What lie is the enemy trying to convince you of? Whatever it is, don't embrace it. Know deep in your soul that God withholds no good thing from you. He has your best interest at heart, now, tomorrow, and forevermore.

Lord, help me to flee when the enemy tries to lead me astray! Amen.

Thoughts
FROM MAMA
by Anita Higman

You know fun when you see it, but as a mama, well, a good time might be something else—like watching you crawl and walk and grow and laugh and play and bloom and succeed, but maybe not the driving away to college part. No, maybe not that...

She Sure Is Persnickety!

As Jesus and the disciples continued on their way to Jerusalem they came to a village where a woman named Martha welcomed them into her home. Her sister Mary sat on the floor, listening to Jesus as He talked. But Martha was the jittery type and was worrying over the big dinner she was preparing. She came to Jesus and said, "Sir, doesn't it seem unfair to You that my sister just sits here while I do all the work? Tell her to come and help me." But the Lord said to her, "Martha, dear friend, you are so upset over all these details! There is really only one thing worth being concerned about. Mary has discovered it— and I won't take it away from her!"

LUKE 10:38–42 (TLB)

There are a lot of Biblical characters that we tend to poke at because they are easy targets when it comes to human flaws. Perhaps some of these faulty folks were added to the Word of God because many of us have similar weaknesses, and we have much we can learn from their failings. One of those people is Martha.

Gotta love that woman. And actually, Jesus *did* love Martha. But she had this persnickety type personality—can we say finicky, fussy, and fastidious?—and she got so fixated on making the festivities perfect that she forgot the main reason they were all there in the first place—Jesus.

MAY WE NOT MISS ANY DIVINE MOMENTS BECAUSE OF OUR FRANTIC WHIRLING. BUT WHEN THAT DOES HAPPEN, JESUS WILL LOVINGLY SAY TO YOU, "MY DEAR FRIEND . . ."

Martha had the Son of God in her living room, but she was too busy in the kitchen with her to-do list to pay close attention. Imagine! We too have the Lord near us. May we not miss any divine moments because of our frantic whirling. But when that does happen, Jesus will lovingly say to you, "My dear friend . . ."

Jesus, may I always keep my focus on what really matters the most . . . You! Amen.

Slow as Molasses

Let the wicked forsake his way,
and the unrighteous man his thoughts;
let him return to the LORD, that he may
have compassion on him, and to our
God, for he will abundantly pardon.
For my thoughts are not your thoughts,
neither are your ways my ways, declares
the LORD. For as the heavens are higher
than the earth, so are my ways higher
than your ways and my thoughts
than your thoughts.

ISAIAH 55:7–9 (ESV)

Have you ever tasted molasses? Some folks say it's good for you. Others say it's delicious. Hard to know for sure since it's hard to pour from the container! You open the bottle, turn it sideways, pat the bottom for encouragement, and, well, it sort of inches out like a slow-moving lava flow. Which is where the old saying came from, "Slow as molasses!" The reason we get annoyed with "slow" is because we live in a society that is pretty unimpressed with that word. We have a need for speed. In fact, we feed on it. We like action and reaction. We want everything—yesterday!

Guess that sort of explains why humans

get so disappointed, confused, and even exasperated with God's timing. He understands our point of view, but we cannot fully comprehend His. God's perspective is eternal, ours is finite. God is all-knowing—we aren't. As the Lord says in Isaiah, "His thoughts aren't like ours, and His ways are not our ways." But what we can also be assured of is that God is always watching out for us, redeeming all things, calming our fears, giving us mercy, and loving us like we've never been loved before.

WE CAN BE ASSURED THAT GOD IS ALWAYS WATCHING OUT FOR US, REDEEMING ALL THINGS, CALMING OUR FEARS, GIVING US MERCY, AND LOVING US LIKE WE'VE NEVER BEEN LOVED BEFORE.

Lord, I don't always understand Your ways, but I choose to trust in You. Amen.

More Nervous Than a Long-Tail Cat in a Room Full of Rocking Chairs!

Therefore I tell you, do not worry about your life, what you will eat or drink; or about your body, what you will wear. Is not life more than food, and the body more than clothes? Look at the birds of the air; they do not sow or reap or store away in barns, and yet your heavenly Father feeds them. Are you not much more valuable than they? Can any one of you by worrying add a single hour to your life?

MATTHEW 6:25–27 (NIV)

From up above, we humans must look like a nervous and puzzling lot. We zip and zoom in cars along winding freeways trying to maneuver ahead of each other, but then on the sidewalks, we move as one, like the migration of the wildebeest in the Serengeti. Maybe we're scared that if we run too far behind we'll get picked off by predators. Perhaps we're running from death. As Christ-followers, we can rest in the peaceful and joyous knowledge that we have life eternal in Christ. And as it says so perfectly in Matthew, the Lord has provided us with all that we need. What a relief! We don't have to chase anything or run from anything or worry about anything.

Does that mean we can sit around and twiddle our thumbs? No, we should be about our Father's business,

WE SHOULD BE ABOUT OUR FATHER'S BUSINESS, BUT AT A PACE THAT ALLOWS US TO BREATHE IN THE GLORIOUS GIFTS WE'VE BEEN GIVEN, HELP OUR FELLOWMAN AS THE HOLY SPIRIT LEADS US, AND DELIGHT IN OUR LOVING AND BEAUTIFUL GOD.

but at a pace that allows us to breathe in the glorious gifts we've been given, help our fellowman as the Holy Spirit leads us, and delight in our loving and beautiful God. It's all about pacing and perspective and our great Provider.

O Lord, I need to step off the world's treadmill of worry. Please give me the courage to follow You in all my comings and goings. Amen.

Nuttier Than a Fruitcake

Words spoken by the wise bring them favor, but the lips of fools consume them. The words of their mouths begin in foolishness, and their talk ends in wicked madness.

ECCLESIASTES 10:12–13 (NRSV)

So, it's Christmastime again, and you love everything about the holiday, right? Yes, God's gift of love. The radiant lights and the fragrant boughs and caroling. It's all wonderful, except for one thing. Just one. When Aunt Willamina brings over her homemade fruitcake. No, please. Anything but that! It's not so much the dryness of the cake that gets to you, but it's those infernal bits of nuts and those candied fruit nodules that lodge in your throat. It's like someone has minced up your child's plastic toys and dumped them in a cake! And you know you're not alone. Lots of other people have dark thoughts about those cakes too. Perhaps that is what helped to spawn the quirky saying, "Nuttier than a fruitcake."

We've all heard that saying, and if we're honest with ourselves, we've all been pretty nutty at times. But there is a step beyond merely being goofy—it's being a fool. Oh dear. Sounds serious. Ecclesiastes gives us a visual that is quite memorable: "The lips of a fool will consume a person." Oh wow. That image will stick like a wedge of candied fruit. But haven't we all seen people who act like this? Hard to watch. What can we do? We should pray for these people, help them, and love them, because someone one of those people might be you or me!

CHRISTMAS IS WONDERFUL, EXCEPT FOR ONE THING. JUST ONE. WHEN AUNT WILLAMINA BRINGS OVER HER HOMEMADE FRUITCAKE. NO, PLEASE. ANYTHING BUT THAT!

Dear God, if I ever get caught in the trap of speaking foolishness, please stop me! I need wisdom in all I do and say. In Jesus' name I pray. Amen.

She Jumped Out of the Frying Pan and into the Fire

Shadrach, Meshach, and Abednego replied, "O Nebuchadnezzar, we do not need to defend ourselves before you. If we are thrown into the blazing furnace, the God whom we serve is able to save us. He will rescue us from your power, Your Majesty. But even if He doesn't, we want to make it clear to you, Your Majesty, that we will never serve your gods or worship the gold statue you have set up."

DANIEL 3:16–18 (NLT)

As you read the full story of Shadrach, Meshach, and Abednego in the Bible, try to imagine it playing out as a movie. What a hair-raising and yet marvelously miraculous story! Since the fall of mankind, life has been hard in general, but these three men were willing to jump from the hot trials of life right into the literal fires of a blazing furnace—all in the name of loyalty to the one true God in whom they trusted fully. Shadrach, Meshach, and Abednego believed God would rescue them, but they said that even if for some reason God didn't choose to save them, they would still go into the furnace rather than follow the king's demands of bowing down to other gods. Not now. Not ever. Those three men were rock solid in their fidelity and faith.

Usually, when we think of the old saying, "Jumping from the frying pan and into the fire," we think of people trying to flee from trouble, only to shockingly discover that they made their situation more dreadful. Shadrach, Meshach, and Abednego knew full well what might happen inside the furnace. They knew, and they entered anyway. But don't miss God's fabulous finale. He comes to their rescue in such an imaginative and theatrical way that Hollywood's best action films would pale in comparison!

DON'T MISS GOD'S FABULOUS FINALE. HE COMES TO THEIR RESCUE IN SUCH AN IMAGINATIVE AND THEATRICAL WAY THAT HOLLYWOOD'S BEST ACTION FILMS WOULD PALE IN COMPARISON!

Lord, like Shadrach, Meshach, and Abednego, may I always be steadfast to You in my fidelity and my faith! Amen.

You're a Day Late and a Dollar Short

We are made right with God
by placing our faith in Jesus Christ.
And this is true for everyone who
believes, no matter who we are.
For everyone has sinned; we all fall
short of God's glorious standard.
Yet God, in His grace, freely makes us
right in His sight. He did this through
Christ Jesus when He freed us from
the penalty for our sins.

ROMANS 3:22–24 (NLT)

Beatrice fell on the bed, completely exhausted. She'd just returned from yet another long day of volunteering. Giving of herself felt good, and people seemed to appreciate her efforts, but sometimes she wondered what her true motivation was. Did she strive endlessly because she still thought of herself as needing to work her way to heaven? Beatrice knew that angle of thinking was not Biblical, and yet she couldn't fully imagine a God offering grace free and clear. There had to be a catch. Then she remembered her pastor speaking on grace and mentioning the Scripture from

Isaiah 64:6, "We have all become like one who is unclean, and all our righteous deeds are like a filthy cloth. We all fade like a leaf, and our iniquities, like the wind, take us away" (NRSV). So Beatrice guessed the verse meant that no matter how hard she tried to make herself good enough for heaven, she would always wind up a day late and a dollar short. Maybe admitting human defeat was the only way to win.

MANKIND IMPRISONS ITSELF IN A THOUSAND WAYS, BUT GOD HOLDS THE KEY— JESUS CHRIST.

At that moment, Beatrice gave up the struggle. She accepted the grace of God though Christ—free and clear—and every muscle in her body relaxed. Her soul found peace. She decided that any volunteering in the future would be done with discernment, and it would be done not with an attitude of climbing to heaven, but one of praising God for making a way for her to get there!

Father God, I realize that mankind imprisons itself in a thousand ways, but You hold the key—Jesus Christ. Amen.

Nip It in the Bud!

*How should we respond to all of this?
Is it good to persist in a life of sin so
that grace may multiply even more?
Absolutely not! How can we die to a life
where sin ruled over us and then invite
sin back into our lives?*

ROMANS 6:1–2 (VOICE)

Hallie was late for work. Again! Traffic was atrocious, and so when she saw a break in the mess, she floored it and sped right on through, running a red light in the process. Okay, that didn't feel so good. Guilt pricked her conscious, but when she saw that no police car was chasing after her, she chose to keep on speeding and weaving through traffic. Once she got too close to another car, and boy, did they honk with a vengeance. But Hallie was on a roll with her offenses, and getting to work quickly became more important than traffic laws, which were there for her own safety and for everyone else's!

Oh dear. Sometimes we get on such a roll with sin that instead of scaring ourselves back into right living, we pick up the pace. Do we ever think, "Why not? After all, it means that grace will only multiply." According to Romans, that is not the way to live as a follower of Christ.

When the Holy Spirit nudges us and lets us know we've done something wrong, we need to repent immediately and move forward.

Maybe a new version of the old saying could be, "When it comes to sinning, girl, nip it in the bud!"

MAYBE A NEW VERSION OF THE OLD SAYING COULD BE, "WHEN IT COMES TO SINNING, GIRL, NIP IT IN THE BUD!"

Holy Spirit, I don't want to keep grieving You with my faults and spiritual frailties. We both know I have many of them. Please show me all the areas of my life that need healing and help and honing, and give me the will and strength to conquer each one! Amen.

You Can't Make a Silk Purse Out of a Sow's Ear

*When someone becomes a Christian,
he becomes a brand new person inside.
He is not the same anymore.
A new life has begun!*

II CORINTHIANS 5:17 (TLB)

There's a witty saying about trying to make a silk purse out of a sow's ear. If you think about that phrase too long, you might stick out your tongue. Sounds pretty disgusting. Probably because when we think of hogs in general, words like smelly, rough, flaky, and hairy come to mind. Nothing even close to the creamy, dreamy feel of a real silk purse. So, you wouldn't even think to use such substandard—not to mention weird—materials to make something so glorious.

This old idiom might make one think of humans trying to make themselves look good and act good and feel good—the way we were before the fall in Eden. But that's utterly impossible too.

On our own, we can't make ourselves into something lovely and useable and glorious—but Jesus can. He can take what had become impossible to work with and make it into something truly beautiful. All we need to do is let Him. Jesus waits for our willingness to repent and accept Him as Lord and Savior—and then to be eager for a supernatural transformation. Philippians 1:6 has some great news when it goes on to remind us, "And I am certain that God, who began the good work within you, will continue His work until it is

ON OUR OWN, WE CAN'T MAKE OURSELVES INTO SOMETHING LOVELY AND USEABLE AND GLORIOUS—BUT JESUS CAN. HE CAN TAKE WHAT HAD BECOME IMPOSSIBLE TO WORK WITH AND MAKE IT INTO SOMETHING TRULY BEAUTIFUL.

finally finished on the day when Christ Jesus returns" (NLT). May we all come to know Him and reply, "Yes, Lord, let the holy beautification of my soul commence!

Lord, please make me into something beautiful for Your glory. I know You want the very best for me always. Amen.

Thoughts
FROM MAMA
by Anita Higman

If you want to win some extra points with me as your mama, then make sure you don't get a sudden twitch in your eye when you see my new hat. Please try your best not to gag on that slice of dry turkey. Oh, and you might want to tread ever-so-lightly when I get a bee in my bonnet!

One Woman's Trash Is Another Woman's Treasure

You are a people holy to the LORD your God. The LORD your God has chosen you to be a people for his treasured possession, out of all the peoples who are on the face of the earth.

DEUTERONOMY 7:6 (ESV)

Some women describe bliss as going to an antique store and coming across a rare find amidst the odds and ends. And then, if she buys that treasure for a song? Well, *ooh là là*! However, the person who sold the treasure might be chuckling all the way to the bank, since she considered that treasure to be pure-o-dee junk. Hence, that old saying, "One woman's trash is another woman's treasure" truly lives on!

But when it comes to the way God feels about the Israelites—and you and me—there is no junk, no trash anywhere. There is only treasure. Nothing complicated. God just wants to be in our lives. That's it. Why? Because of His love for us. Psalm 139:13-16 says it so exquisitely, "You made all the delicate, inner parts of my body and knit them together in my mother's womb. Thank You for making me so wonderfully complex! It is amazing to think about. Your workmanship is marvelous—and how well I know it. You were there while I was being formed in utter seclusion! You saw me before I was born and scheduled each day of my life before I began to breathe. Every day was recorded in Your book!" (TLB)

MAY WE EMBRACE GOD'S LOVE FULLY, RETURN IT BOLDLY, AND LIVE IN THE SWEET KNOWLEDGE OF IT DAILY!

How lovely to be so loved by our Creator. May we no longer need to keep questioning God's love for us. May we embrace His love fully, return it boldly, and live in the sweet knowledge of it daily!

Lord Jesus, when I get beat down by this world it is easy to think even You are against me. May I always know deep in my soul of Your great love for me. Amen.

Don't Count Your Chickens before They Hatch

When someone invites you to a wedding feast, do not take the place of honor, for a person more distinguished than you may have been invited. If so, the host who invited both of you will come and say to you, "Give this person your seat." Then, humiliated, you will have to take the least important place. But when you are invited, take the lowest place, so that when your host comes, he will say to you, "Friend, move up to a better place." Then you will be honored in the presence of all the other guests. For all those who exalt themselves will be humbled, and those who humble themselves will be exalted.

LUKE 14:8–11 (NIV)

Sometimes we like to intensely focus on our future plans, but sometimes we don't have all the info. We get ahead of ourselves. The old saying about counting our chickens is a good one in that sometimes after prayer we just need to see how life will unfold day by day—that is, trusting God for the best in all circumstances, but trusting Him all the way through, even when prayers don't get answered exactly as we want them.

In Luke we are told of another instance where humans can get ahead of themselves. People who might think they deserve to be in the place of honor at a wedding banquet, for instance. But those same folks may be in for a rude awakening, since they may be asked to move to the back. Talk about humiliation. And in front of everybody present. Yikes! Much better to think of ourselves in lowly terms so that we might be exalted.

HOW SHOULD A CHRIST-FOLLOWER LIVE THEN? WALK HUMBLY WITH OUR GOD? AH, YES. COULD ANYTHING BE MORE PERFECT, COULD ANYTHING BE MORE BEAUTIFUL?

How should a Christ-follower live then? Walk humbly with our God? Ah, yes. Could anything be more perfect, could anything be more beautiful?

Lord, may I always walk humbly with You by my side. Amen.

You Can't Squeeze Blood Out of a Turnip

Jesus said to his disciples, "Truly, I say to you, only with difficulty will a rich person enter the kingdom of heaven. Again I tell you, it is easier for a camel to go through the eye of a needle than for a rich person to enter the kingdom of God." When the disciples heard this, they were greatly astonished, saying, "Who then can be saved?" But Jesus looked at them and said, "With man this is impossible, but with God all things are possible."

MATTHEW 19:23–26 (ESV)

The first time you hear the old saying, "You can't squeeze blood out of a turnip," you might blink a few times. That visual doesn't quite add up. Of course, when you squash or dice or toss a turnip into a blender, you won't get anything but turnip puree! Nor can anyone pay off a debt if he or she has no money in the bank. These are both impossibilities. And that is just what Jesus was saying to His disciples when they first discussed the rich young ruler. Jesus told them that it would be easier for a camel to make it through the eye of a needle than for a rich person to enter God's kingdom. Who could be saved then? "It would indeed be impossible on our own," Jesus said. But He went on to say that what is impossible for man isn't impossible for God.

BUT NOT TO WORRY; WITH OUR GOD, ALL THINGS ARE POSSIBLE. THAT PROMISE WILL HELP US TO SLEEP MORE DEEPLY, LIVE MORE FULLY, AND LOVE LIKE WE MEAN IT!

We have that beautiful hope. Not just concerning salvation and heaven, but everything. We live in a world that will try to slow us down, trip us up, or stop us cold. But not to worry; with our God, all things are possible. That promise will help us to sleep more deeply, live more fully, and love like we mean it!

Lord, thank You for Your words of truth that give me such hope! Amen.

Stop That Lollygagging!

*Whoever works his land will have plenty
of bread, but he who follows worthless
pursuits will have plenty of poverty.
A faithful man will abound with
blessings, but whoever hastens
to be rich will not go unpunished.*

PROVERBS 28:19–20 (ESV)

Yep, you were headed off to get your
mama a jar of green beans from the
cellar when you were waylaid with a dozen
more interesting activities along the way.
You know, picking the lint off your sweater.
Playing with the stinkbug that was creeping
its way along the stone floor. Maybe
rechecking all the dates on the canning
jars and arranging the rows to look more
uniform. Hey, that last one is important!

You hated to admit it, but you knew you
could raise up idling to an art form. So, when
Mama hollered out to you with, "Stop that
lollygagging!" you knew you'd been caught
loafing and been duly reprimanded.

Well, the Bible also contains some mama-
like warnings and reprimands concerning
the twiddling of one's thumbs, whether
you're a child or an adult. Proverbs 6:6–11
doesn't beat around the bush when it states
with a touch of wit, "You lazy fool, look at

an ant. Watch it closely; let it teach you a thing or two. Nobody has to tell it what to do. All summer it stores up food; at harvest it stockpiles provisions. So how long are you going to laze around doing nothing? How long before you get out of bed? A nap here, a nap there, a day off here, a day off there, sit back, take it easy—do you **SO, WHEN MAMA HOLLERED OUT TO YOU WITH, "STOP THAT LOLLYGAGGING!" YOU KNEW YOU'D BEEN CAUGHT LOAFING AND BEEN DULY REPRIMANDED.** know what comes next? Just this: You can look forward to a dirt-poor life, poverty your permanent houseguest!" (THE MESSAGE)

Wow, even Mama didn't think to say all that!

Dear Lord, sometimes I get into a rut doing either too much or too little. Please show me how to have a godly balance in all areas of my life. Amen.

You Look Bright-Eyed and Bushy-Tailed

Jesus said to her, "Did I not tell you that if you believed, you would see the glory of God?" So they took away the stone. And Jesus looked upward and said, "Father, I thank You for having heard Me. I knew that You always hear Me, but I have said this for the sake of the crowd standing here, so that they may believe that You sent Me." When He had said this, He cried with a loud voice, "Lazarus, come out!" The dead man came out, his hands and feet bound with strips of cloth, and his face wrapped in a cloth. Jesus said to them, "Unbind him, and let him go."

JOHN 11:40–44 (NRSV)

If you've read the story about Jesus raising Lazarus from the dead, you've surely tried to imagine this scene as it plays out. The story is no less than epic. It makes one wonder what happened after Lazarus's friends undid his cloth wrappings and his face was exposed. Lazarus may have had an expression of shock or bafflement. Then again—maybe the man bypassed those more stupefied emotions and instead looked positively bright-eyed and bushy-tailed!

When we accept Christ and we go from spiritual death to life, perhaps we should all feel some of that get-up-and-go. You know, some of that alertness and eagerness to take on the world for Christ. After all, what was lost is now found. What was without truth and purpose is awakened to all the joys of life in Christ, including the splendor of heaven!

AFTER ALL, WHAT WAS LOST IS NOW FOUND. WHAT WAS WITHOUT TRUTH AND PURPOSE IS AWAKENED TO ALL THE JOYS OF LIFE IN CHRIST, INCLUDING THE SPLENDOR OF HEAVEN!

Heavenly Father, sometimes I get so comfortable with my Christianity, I forget the real glories of what I have in You . . . the peace that goes beyond my understanding, the love You shower on me, and the promise of eternal life. Please renew in me the excitement of living out this good news and sharing it with others. In Jesus' holy name I pray. Amen.

I've Got Bigger Fish to Fry

While bodily training is of some value, godliness is of value in every way, as it holds promise for the present life and also for the life to come.

1 TIMOTHY 4:8 (ESV)

When people are young, they find a lot of creative ways to waste time. After all, they get the feeling they will live forever—or close enough. So, they find ingenious ways to use time perhaps unwisely. They might count kitchen floor tiles, look up meaningless data online, text to say hello for the zillionth time, recount the kitchen floor tiles—just to make sure—or they may take oodles of selfies. Hey, gotta look good on social media! People like to stay busy, but some busyness eventually morphs into a colossal waste of time.

The older people get the more and more focused they tend to get. Like Mama, they might say, "I've got bigger fish to fry." We might also start to ask the harder questions of life like, "Have I loved God and mankind with my whole heart? Do I know the will of God? What can I do to thank the Lord for all He's done for me?"

As the Bible says, "While bodily training is of some value, godliness is of value in every way, as it holds promise for the present life and also for the life to come" (ESV). So, there are many good activities, including exercise, that we can partake of, but it would be wise to always ask God what He would like us to do with the hours He's given us and to remember that godliness is of value in every way.

WISDOM WOULD BE TO ASK GOD WHAT HE WOULD LIKE US TO DO WITH THE HOURS HE'S GIVEN US AND TO REMEMBER THAT GODLINESS IS OF VALUE IN EVERY WAY.

Dear God, I want to be all that You created me to be. Please show me how to use my time wisely. In Jesus' name I pray. Amen.

Don't Make Me Come Over There!

In the fourth watch of the night he came to them, walking on the sea. But when the disciples saw him walking on the sea, they were terrified, and said, "It is a ghost!" and they cried out in fear. But immediately Jesus spoke to them, saying, "Take heart; it is I. Do not be afraid." And Peter answered him, "Lord, if it is you, command me to come to you on the water." He said, "Come." So Peter got out of the boat and walked on the water and came to Jesus. But when he saw the wind, he was afraid, and beginning to sink he cried out, "Lord, save me." Jesus immediately reached out his hand and took hold of him, saying to him, "O you of little faith, why did you doubt?"

MATTHEW 14:25–31 (ESV)

Mamas sometimes reach their limits, and one way you'll know is when you hear her bellow, "Don't make me come over there!" That means you are in trouble, and you had best cease and desist whatever you are doing wrong, or she will come over to offer you some firmer encouragement to stop! Mamas love us, and one of the ways we can love them back is to take them at their word and just do what they say.

In Matthew, when Peter got the idea that he too could walk on water, the Lord asked him to come. Peter did miraculously walk on water, but the moment he took his eyes off Christ, he became fearful and faltered in his faith. Even though Jesus did "come over there" to keep Peter from drowning, He really wanted Peter to keep the faith and keep doing what all the world called impossible.

> YES, THE LORD LOVED PETER—AS HE LOVES YOU AND ME—BUT ONE OF THE WAYS WE CAN LOVE HIM BACK IS TO TAKE HIM AT HIS WORD AND JUST DO WHAT HE SAYS!

Yes, the Lord loved Peter—as He loves you and me—but one of the ways we can love Him back is to take Him at His word and just do what He says!

Lord, give me faith to do the impossible! Amen.

Can't Trust Her as Far as You Can Throw Her

Strength and dignity are her clothing, and she laughs at the time to come. She opens her mouth with wisdom, and the teaching of kindness is on her tongue. She looks well to the ways of her household and does not eat the bread of idleness. Her children rise up and call her blessed; her husband also, and he praises her: "Many women have done excellently, but you surpass them all."

PROVERBS 31:25–29 (ESV)

The concept of integrity is beautiful. So beautiful, in fact, maybe we'd like to see a lot more of it! Perhaps that is one reason people created sayings like "Can't trust her as far as you can throw her." When we do think back on integrity, it reminds us of truthfulness and honor, loyalty and decency. What excellent and inspiring ideals.

Yes, people might like to have integrity—like they possess other things. After all, it would look good on one's spiritual resume! But people can be disappointing. They tend to say one thing and do another. We all have a tendency to watch out for ourselves. At times we can even be a muddled mess of mendacity!

But God is good. He not only loves us dearly, but He loves us enough to help us get out of our own way spiritually! With the help of the Holy Spirit, we can indeed be better women of God. The Lord already sees the potential in us, and it is sublime. Shall we let Him help us with that glorious goal?

Father God, make me into a Proverbs 31 kind of woman. I am ready and willing. Please let the beautification of my soul begin! In Jesus' powerful name I pray. Amen.

It'll All Come Out
in the Wash

*Do not be anxious about anything,
but in everything by prayer and
supplication with thanksgiving let your
requests be made known to God. And
the peace of God, which surpasses all
understanding, will guard your hearts
and your minds in Christ Jesus.*

PHILIPPIANS 4:6–7 (ESV)

The little gal, Zoe, was a chip off the old block when it came to making messes like her mama. The mother-daughter duo could be a good two feet away from a plate of spaghetti and somehow it would wind up on the front of their clothes. Sometimes the incidents defied the laws of nature. In fact, the mother had gotten so used to her little girl's (and her own) messes that it became funny—almost. One day Zoe jumped into a pile of autumn leaves just for fun. Just below the surface, though, was a pool of deep gooey mud. Zoe got covered. Her face. Her new outfit. Her school backpack. Her lunch pail. Only thing that didn't get hit was the inside of her socks. Zoe's mom wanted to cry or yell, but instead she decided to laugh. The mom knew she would have a hard time reprimanding her little gal since her own new blouse was already sporting a chimichanga stain! She chuckled again and told Zoe, "No worries. It'll all come out in the wash."

Then that same mom was wise enough to turn the muddy affair into a teachable moment, reminding Zoe that the way to a better life as a Jesus follower was to not give in to worry and anxiousness. Did

> SHE CHUCKLED AGAIN AND TOLD ZOE, "NO WORRIES. IT'LL ALL COME OUT IN THE WASH!

that mean Zoe could now make even bigger messes just for fun? No, but it meant that whatever life handed them both, they could pray about it and trust God. No matter what. Nuff said.

Dearest Lord, I admit I can be such a mess sometimes. And even when I get my attitude and actions right, life still throws me for a loop sometimes. Please help me to pray and leave my worries in Your capable and powerful hands. Then may the peace that passes all understanding be mine. Amen.

Great Day in the Morning!

In the morning, LORD,
You hear my voice;
in the morning I lay my requests
before You and wait expectantly.

PSALM 5:3 (NIV)

One old and amusing saying used to be, "Great day in the morning!" Perhaps this phrase got used so much through the years, you and your family no longer know exactly what it means anymore. But one thing it could represent is that literally you're anticipating a fine morning. And why not?

Every day is your best day when you know God's love. Will all our earthly ducks be in a pretty row? Not gonna happen. Will God be with us, no matter what? Yes. We have that guarantee. Joshua 1:9 promises each of us, "Have I not commanded you? Be strong and courageous. Do not be frightened, and do not be dismayed, for the LORD your God is with you wherever you go" (ESV).

And in Matthew we are also reminded, "And behold, I am with you always, to the end of the age" (28:20 ESV). In fact, the very word Immanuel means "God with us."

May this be a deep comfort to us as we wait for our first glorious breath of heaven!

Yes, in the Lord's daily presence there is an abundance for the heart and soul that cannot be matched on earth. A beauty that cannot be reproduced, even though we try. And a promise that will continually give us enough hope to keep us rising up in the morning. To praise. To know. To share the miracle of life with God.

YES, IN THE LORD'S DAILY PRESENCE THERE IS AN ABUNDANCE FOR THE HEART AND SOUL THAT CANNOT BE MATCHED ON EARTH. A BEAUTY THAT CANNOT BE REPRODUCED, EVEN THOUGH WE TRY. AND A PROMISE THAT WILL CONTINUALLY GIVE US ENOUGH HOPE TO KEEP US RISING UP IN THE MORNING.

Lord Jesus, may I always be happy deep in my soul even when the whole world seems to be falling apart. May I always have joy in You. Amen.

Thoughts
FROM MAMA
by Anita Higman

There are countless
mama-moments that
are special, but the best
one of all is when I
see you growing up to
be all that God wants
you to be. Yeah, that
is the mama-moment
that makes my soul sing
the hallelujah chorus!

LIVE YOUR FAITH

Dear Friend,

This book was prayerfully crafted with you, the reader, in mind—every word, every sentence, every page—was thoughtfully written, designed, and packaged to encourage you...right where you are this very moment. At DaySpring, our vision is to see every person experience the life-changing message of God's love. So, as we worked through rough drafts, design changes, edits and details, we prayed for you to deeply experience His unfailing love, indescribable peace, and pure joy. It is our sincere hope that through these Truth-filled pages your heart will be blessed, knowing that God cares about you—your desires and disappointments, your challenges and dreams.

He knows. He cares. He loves you unconditionally.

BLESSINGS!
THE DAYSPRING BOOK TEAM

**Additional copies of this book and
other DaySpring titles can be purchased
at fine retailers everywhere.
Order online at <u>dayspring.com</u>
or
by phone at 1-877-751-4347**

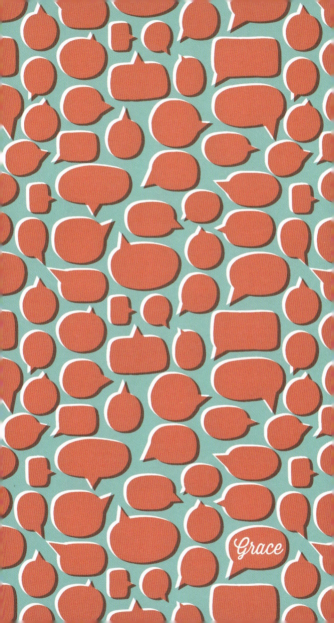

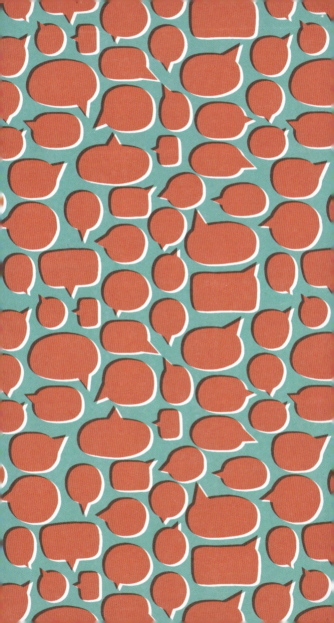